How to be a Grammar Nazi
for Geniuses

By William Bullokar

™

www.justforgeniuses.com

DISCLAIMER: The book is a work of parody. Nothing in this book is meant to imply any facts about any actual persons or entities.

All rights reserved. No part of this publication may be reproduced, distributed, or transmitted in any form or by any means, including photocopying, recording, or other electronic or mechanical methods, without the prior written permission of the publisher.

Copyright © 2014 by Westlake Gavin Publishers LLC

Just for Geniuses, For Geniuses, and accompanying logos are trademarks of Westlake Gavin Publishers LLC and may not be used without written permission. All other trademarks are the property of their respective owners. Westlake Gavin Publishers LLC, is not associated with any other product or service mentioned in this book.

HUMANS OF MIRTH COLLECTION   TGGT1004

Library of *Con*-gress Cataloging-in-Publication Data

How to be a Grammar Nazi for Geniuses / by William Bullokar
p. cm.
ISBN 978-1-63231-997-5
1. Bullokar, William   2. Parody, imitations, etc.   I. Title.

First Edition

10 9 8 7 6 5 4 3 2 1

Inside...

Learn every obscure grammar rule. You never know when they will come in handy!

Best techniques to annoy family, friends, and colleagues.

Getting bored with just grammar? Add spelling to your repertoire.

Why typing on a mobile device is no excuse for poor grammar and/or spelling.

Learn to recognize trolls who purposely make mistakes to bait and harass you. (You know they only do that because they're jealous.)

And so much more...

How to be a Grammar Nazi *for Geniuses*

You should be ashamed of yourself. Wanting to be a Grammar Nazi is not something to be proud of. Grammar Nazis are the scourge of the Earth and should be tortured by making lot's of misteaks by purpose until they renounce they're evil ways.

How to be a Grammar Nazi *for Geniuses*

You should be ashamed of yourself. Wanting to be a Grammar Nazi is not something to be proud of. Grammar Nazis are the scourge of the Earth and should be tortured by making lot's of misteaks by purpose until they renounce they're evil ways.

Read enough? Turn to page 104

How to be a Grammar Nazi *for Geniuses*

You should be ashamed of yourself. Wanting to be a Grammar Nazi is not something to be proud of. Grammar Nazis are the scourge of the Earth and should be tortured by making lot's of misteaks by purpose until they renounce they're evil ways.

Read enough? Turn to page 104

How to be a Grammar Nazi *for Geniuses*

You should be ashamed of yourself. Wanting to be a Grammar Nazi is not something to be proud of. Grammar Nazis are the scourge of the Earth and should be tortured by making lot's of misteaks by purpose until they renounce they're evil ways.

Read enough? Turn to page 104

How to be a Grammar Nazi *for Geniuses*

You should be ashamed of yourself. Wanting to be a Grammar Nazi is not something to be proud of. Grammar Nazis are the scourge of the Earth and should be tortured by making lot's of misteaks by purpose until they renounce they're evil ways.

Read enough? Turn to page 104

How to be a Grammar Nazi *for Geniuses*

You should be ashamed of yourself. Wanting to be a Grammar Nazi is not something to be proud of. Grammar Nazis are the scourge of the Earth and should be tortured by making lot's of misteaks by purpose until they renounce they're evil ways.

Read enough? Turn to page 104

How to be a Grammar Nazi *for Geniuses*

You should be ashamed of yourself. Wanting to be a Grammar Nazi is not something to be proud of. Grammar Nazis are the scourge of the Earth and should be tortured by making lot's of misteaks by purpose until they renounce they're evil ways.

Read enough? Turn to page 104

How to be a Grammar Nazi *for Geniuses*

You should be ashamed of yourself. Wanting to be a Grammar Nazi is not something to be proud of. Grammar Nazis are the scourge of the Earth and should be tortured by making lot's of misteaks by purpose until they renounce they're evil ways.

Read enough? Turn to page 104

How to be a Grammar Nazi *for Geniuses*

How to be a Grammar Nazi *for Geniuses*

You should be ashamed of yourself. Wanting to be a Grammar Nazi is not something to be proud of. Grammar Nazis are the scourge of the Earth and should be tortured by making lot's of misteaks by purpose until they renounce they're evil ways.

Read enough? Turn to page 104

How to be a Grammar Nazi *for Geniuses*

You should be ashamed of yourself. Wanting to be a Grammar Nazi is not something to be proud of. Grammar Nazis are the scourge of the Earth and should be tortured by making lot's of misteaks by purpose until they renounce they're evil ways.

Read enough? Turn to page 104

How to be a Grammar Nazi *for Geniuses*

How to be a Grammar Nazi *for Geniuses*

You should be ashamed of yourself. Wanting to be a Grammar Nazi is not something to be proud of. Grammar Nazis are the scourge of the Earth and should be tortured by making lot's of misteaks by purpose until they renounce they're evil ways.

Read enough? Turn to page 104

How to be a Grammar Nazi *for Geniuses*

You should be ashamed of yourself. Wanting to be a Grammar Nazi is not something to be proud of. Grammar Nazis are the scourge of the Earth and should be tortured by making lot's of misteaks by purpose until they renounce they're evil ways.

Read enough? Turn to page 104

How to be a Grammar Nazi *for Geniuses*

You should be ashamed of yourself. Wanting to be a Grammar Nazi is not something to be proud of. Grammar Nazis are the scourge of the Earth and should be tortured by making lot's of misteaks by purpose until they renounce they're evil ways.

Read enough? Turn to page 104

You should be ashamed of yourself. Wanting to be a Grammar Nazi is not something to be proud of. Grammar Nazis are the scourge of the Earth and should be tortured by making lot's of misteaks by purpose until they renounce they're evil ways.

Read enough? Turn to page 104

How to be a Grammar Nazi *for Geniuses*

You should be ashamed of yourself. Wanting to be a Grammar Nazi is not something to be proud of. Grammar Nazis are the scourge of the Earth and should be tortured by making lot's of misteaks by purpose until they renounce they're evil ways.

Read enough? Turn to page 104

How to be a Grammar Nazi *for Geniuses*

You should be ashamed of yourself. Wanting to be a Grammar Nazi is not something to be proud of. Grammar Nazis are the scourge of the Earth and should be tortured by making lot's of misteaks by purpose until they renounce they're evil ways.

Read enough? Turn to page 104

You should be ashamed of yourself. Wanting to be a Grammar Nazi is not something to be proud of. Grammar Nazis are the scourge of the Earth and should be tortured by making lot's of misteaks by purpose until they renounce they're evil ways.

Read enough? Turn to page 104

You should be ashamed of yourself. Wanting to be a Grammar Nazi is not something to be proud of. Grammar Nazis are the scourge of the Earth and should be tortured by making lot's of misteaks by purpose until they renounce they're evil ways.

Read enough? Turn to page 104

How to be a Grammar Nazi *for Geniuses*

You should be ashamed of yourself. Wanting to be a Grammar Nazi is not something to be proud of. Grammar Nazis are the scourge of the Earth and should be tortured by making lot's of misteaks by purpose until they renounce they're evil ways.

Read enough? Turn to page 104

How to be a Grammar Nazi *for Geniuses*

You should be ashamed of yourself. Wanting to be a Grammar Nazi is not something to be proud of. Grammar Nazis are the scourge of the Earth and should be tortured by making lot's of misteaks by purpose until they renounce they're evil ways.

Read enough? Turn to page 104

How to be a Grammar Nazi *for Geniuses*

You should be ashamed of yourself. Wanting to be a Grammar Nazi is not something to be proud of. Grammar Nazis are the scourge of the Earth and should be tortured by making lot's of misteaks by purpose until they renounce they're evil ways.

Read enough? Turn to page 104

How to be a Grammar Nazi *for Geniuses*

You should be ashamed of yourself. Wanting to be a Grammar Nazi is not something to be proud of. Grammar Nazis are the scourge of the Earth and should be tortured by making lot's of misteaks by purpose until they renounce they're evil ways.

Read enough? Turn to page 104

How to be a Grammar Nazi *for Geniuses*

You should be ashamed of yourself. Wanting to be a Grammar Nazi is not something to be proud of. Grammar Nazis are the scourge of the Earth and should be tortured by making lot's of misteaks by purpose until they renounce they're evil ways.

Read enough? Turn to page 104

How to be a Grammar Nazi *for Geniuses*

You should be ashamed of yourself. Wanting to be a Grammar Nazi is not something to be proud of. Grammar Nazis are the scourge of the Earth and should be tortured by making lot's of misteaks by purpose until they renounce they're evil ways.

Read enough? Turn to page 104

How to be a Grammar Nazi *for Geniuses*

You should be ashamed of yourself. Wanting to be a Grammar Nazi is not something to be proud of. Grammar Nazis are the scourge of the Earth and should be tortured by making lot's of misteaks by purpose until they renounce they're evil ways.

Read enough? Turn to page 104

How to be a Grammar Nazi *for Geniuses*

You should be ashamed of yourself. Wanting to be a Grammar Nazi is not something to be proud of. Grammar Nazis are the scourge of the Earth and should be tortured by making lot's of misteaks by purpose until they renounce they're evil ways.

Read enough? Turn to page 104

How to be a Grammar Nazi *for Geniuses*

You should be ashamed of yourself. Wanting to be a Grammar Nazi is not something to be proud of. Grammar Nazis are the scourge of the Earth and should be tortured by making lot's of misteaks by purpose until they renounce they're evil ways.

Read enough? Turn to page 104

How to be a Grammar Nazi *for Geniuses*

You should be ashamed of yourself. Wanting to be a Grammar Nazi is not something to be proud of. Grammar Nazis are the scourge of the Earth and should be tortured by making lot's of misteaks by purpose until they renounce they're evil ways.

Read enough? Turn to page 104

How to be a Grammar Nazi *for Geniuses*

You should be ashamed of yourself. Wanting to be a Grammar Nazi is not something to be proud of. Grammar Nazis are the scourge of the Earth and should be tortured by making lot's of misteaks by purpose until they renounce they're evil ways.

Read enough? Turn to page 104

How to be a Grammar Nazi *for Geniuses*

You should be ashamed of yourself. Wanting to be a Grammar Nazi is not something to be proud of. Grammar Nazis are the scourge of the Earth and should be tortured by making lot's of misteaks by purpose until they renounce they're evil ways.

Read enough? Turn to page 104

How to be a Grammar Nazi *for Geniuses*

You should be ashamed of yourself. Wanting to be a Grammar Nazi is not something to be proud of. Grammar Nazis are the scourge of the Earth and should be tortured by making lot's of misteaks by purpose until they renounce they're evil ways.

Read enough? Turn to page 104

How to be a Grammar Nazi *for Geniuses*

You should be ashamed of yourself. Wanting to be a Grammar Nazi is not something to be proud of. Grammar Nazis are the scourge of the Earth and should be tortured by making lot's of misteaks by purpose until they renounce they're evil ways.

Read enough? Turn to page 104

How to be a Grammar Nazi *for Geniuses*

You should be ashamed of yourself. Wanting to be a Grammar Nazi is not something to be proud of. Grammar Nazis are the scourge of the Earth and should be tortured by making lot's of misteaks by purpose until they renounce they're evil ways.

Read enough? Turn to page 104

How to be a Grammar Nazi *for Geniuses*

You should be ashamed of yourself. Wanting to be a Grammar Nazi is not something to be proud of. Grammar Nazis are the scourge of the Earth and should be tortured by making lot's of misteaks by purpose until they renounce they're evil ways.

Read enough? Turn to page 104

How to be a Grammar Nazi *for Geniuses*

You should be ashamed of yourself. Wanting to be a Grammar Nazi is not something to be proud of. Grammar Nazis are the scourge of the Earth and should be tortured by making lot's of misteaks by purpose until they renounce they're evil ways.

Read enough? Turn to page 104

How to be a Grammar Nazi *for Geniuses*

You should be ashamed of yourself. Wanting to be a Grammar Nazi is not something to be proud of. Grammar Nazis are the scourge of the Earth and should be tortured by making lot's of misteaks by purpose until they renounce they're evil ways.

Read enough? Turn to page 104

How to be a Grammar Nazi *for Geniuses*

You should be ashamed of yourself. Wanting to be a Grammar Nazi is not something to be proud of. Grammar Nazis are the scourge of the Earth and should be tortured by making lot's of misteaks by purpose until they renounce they're evil ways.

Read enough? Turn to page 104

How to be a Grammar Nazi *for Geniuses*

You should be ashamed of yourself. Wanting to be a Grammar Nazi is not something to be proud of. Grammar Nazis are the scourge of the Earth and should be tortured by making lot's of misteaks by purpose until they renounce they're evil ways.

Read enough? Turn to page 104

How to be a Grammar Nazi *for Geniuses*

You should be ashamed of yourself. Wanting to be a Grammar Nazi is not something to be proud of. Grammar Nazis are the scourge of the Earth and should be tortured by making lot's of misteaks by purpose until they renounce they're evil ways.

Read enough? Turn to page 104

How to be a Grammar Nazi *for Geniuses*

You should be ashamed of yourself. Wanting to be a Grammar Nazi is not something to be proud of. Grammar Nazis are the scourge of the Earth and should be tortured by making lot's of misteaks by purpose until they renounce they're evil ways.

Read enough? Turn to page 104

How to be a Grammar Nazi *for Geniuses*

You should be ashamed of yourself. Wanting to be a Grammar Nazi is not something to be proud of. Grammar Nazis are the scourge of the Earth and should be tortured by making lot's of misteaks by purpose until they renounce they're evil ways.

Read enough? Turn to page 104

How to be a Grammar Nazi *for Geniuses*

You should be ashamed of yourself. Wanting to be a Grammar Nazi is not something to be proud of. Grammar Nazis are the scourge of the Earth and should be tortured by making lot's of misteaks by purpose until they renounce they're evil ways.

Read enough? Turn to page 104

How to be a Grammar Nazi *for Geniuses*

You should be ashamed of yourself. Wanting to be a Grammar Nazi is not something to be proud of. Grammar Nazis are the scourge of the Earth and should be tortured by making lot's of misteaks by purpose until they renounce they're evil ways.

Read enough? Turn to page 104

How to be a Grammar Nazi *for Geniuses*

You should be ashamed of yourself. Wanting to be a Grammar Nazi is not something to be proud of. Grammar Nazis are the scourge of the Earth and should be tortured by making lot's of misteaks by purpose until they renounce they're evil ways.

Read enough? Turn to page 104

How to be a Grammar Nazi *for Geniuses*

You should be ashamed of yourself. Wanting to be a Grammar Nazi is not something to be proud of. Grammar Nazis are the scourge of the Earth and should be tortured by making lot's of misteaks by purpose until they renounce they're evil ways.

Read enough? Turn to page 104

How to be a Grammar Nazi *for Geniuses*

You should be ashamed of yourself. Wanting to be a Grammar Nazi is not something to be proud of. Grammar Nazis are the scourge of the Earth and should be tortured by making lot's of misteaks by purpose until they renounce they're evil ways.

Read enough? Turn to page 104

How to be a Grammar Nazi *for Geniuses*

You should be ashamed of yourself. Wanting to be a Grammar Nazi is not something to be proud of. Grammar Nazis are the scourge of the Earth and should be tortured by making lot's of misteaks by purpose until they renounce they're evil ways.

Read enough? Turn to page 104

How to be a Grammar Nazi *for Geniuses*

You should be ashamed of yourself. Wanting to be a Grammar Nazi is not something to be proud of. Grammar Nazis are the scourge of the Earth and should be tortured by making lot's of misteaks by purpose until they renounce they're evil ways.

Read enough? Turn to page 104

How to be a Grammar Nazi *for Geniuses*

You should be ashamed of yourself. Wanting to be a Grammar Nazi is not something to be proud of. Grammar Nazis are the scourge of the Earth and should be tortured by making lot's of misteaks by purpose until they renounce they're evil ways.

Read enough? Turn to page 104

How to be a Grammar Nazi *for Geniuses*

You should be ashamed of yourself. Wanting to be a Grammar Nazi is not something to be proud of. Grammar Nazis are the scourge of the Earth and should be tortured by making lot's of misteaks by purpose until they renounce they're evil ways.

Read enough? Turn to page 104

Yep, that's it. That's the whole book.

Honestly, how many more times do we need to repeat it? If fifty times is not enough, we suggest you read the book again. As many times as it takes. **Until you repent.**

You got the point right away? That's wonderful news, but not surprising. After all… you are a Genius!

 Use it as a notebook to jot down all the times you successfully refrained from correcting another person's grammar. (The left sided pages have been lined for your convenience.)

 "Gift it forward" Give the book to an unsuspecting friend, family member, or colleague—and help save the world from the scourge of Grammar Nazism.

 Add it to your *Just for Geniuses*™ collection. No promises, but serious collectors are expecting the value of all *Just for Geniuses*™ branded merchandise to substantially rise in the decades and centuries ahead.

We couldn't write books like this without readers like you to support us. Any feedback you give would be greatly appreciated. We have fragile egos, so be gentle about it. Or funny. Just be damn well sure you use correct grammar or else we will have a field day with you!

Please give us feedback at
www.justforgeniuses.com/feedback

How to be a Grammar Nazi *for Geniuses*

Sorry to hear that. But don't despair. The real power of the *Just for Geniuses*™ brand is the flexibility and the ability to customize it **to your needs**. Think gifts, collectibles, promos, charity fund-raising, corporate events, advocacy, and much more.

Depending on your needs, we have the perfect solution for you:

- Submit a customization request to our design team at no cost. (We will try to accommodate everyone's request based on our discretion.)
- Ask our Professional Services team to assist you (minimum order applies.) This is necessary for time-sensitive requests.
- License *Just for Geniuses*™ for your product, service, or media needs. This would give you the most flexibility.

What are you waiting for? Submit your request today at **www.justforgeniuses.com/solutions**

How to be a Grammar Nazi *for Geniuses*

www.justforgeniuses.com

www.ingramcontent.com/pod-product-compliance
Lightning Source LLC
Chambersburg PA
CBHW070854050426
42453CB00012B/2188